A NIGHT IN

or

A Struggle for Life o

by

Rev. E. Donald Carr

A new edition of the original account of 1865

with editorial notes by Andrew Jenkinson

Contents

Acknowledgements

The main author remains, of course, the Reverend E. Donald Carr, without whose story there would be no book; but as editor I am indebted to Hilary Clark for passing on to us the text of her last edition. Also to those who have enabled us to embellish this new edition with illustrations: Gerald Newton for the cover and fly-leaf; my wife Gill for the drawings of the two churches, the hare and the boots. The story and its historical context has been discussed with several people including the present incumbents of the groups of parishes which embrace Woolstaston and Ratlinghope respectively, with Ian Langford of Ratlinghope and Tony Carr of the Shropshire Record Office. Thanks to all who have helped to shed light on the story and encouraged us to keep it in print.

Publisher's Preface

Scenesetters are pleased to publish a new edition of Rev. Donald Carr's epic account of his survival when he was lost over-night in a violent snowstorm in 1865. Rev. Carr was quick to publish the first account himself in April 1865, devoting any profits on its sale to restoration work on his church at Wolstaston.

We first came across this true tale of endurance and dedication to duty soon after our arrival in Shropshire. It had just been republished in 1970 by a local printer. The flyleaf claimed it to be based on the eighth edition, dated 1931. However, the oldest edition in the Local Studies Library in Shrewsbury is the eighth, and that was published before 1907 by James Nisbet & Co of London. "A new edition", un-numbered, was published by The Stretton Press of Sandford Avenue, Church Stretton in 1917. This carried a photograph of Rev. Carr and two views of the Long Mynd. Clearly the story was, and still is, very popular, passing through a number of slightly different formats. We cannot accurately tell what number this edition should bear!

The wording of the earliest known version was used most recently by Clarke and Howard Books of Wolverhampton in their edition of 1985, and that is followed here. We have retained the additional account by Rev. Carr of "The Snowstorm of 1865". This was written in 1887 or 1888 as a separate note, but seems not to have appeared with the main story until added as a preface in the 1970 edition.

We have taken the liberty of adding a few illustrations to the original account and some footnotes to explain or update the factual information given by Rev. Carr. In many respects the Long Mynd has changed little in the past 130 years. It remains a wide, high expanse of heather clad moorland. Although today most visitors see it as an area of beautiful open countryside, preserved for posterity through its ownership by the National Trust, its importance to the local farmers is still as an area of common grazing for their sheep and a few ponies.

Access to the hill has improved, with the metalling of both the Burway from Church Stretton to Ratlinghope and the lanes across the north end of the hill from All Stretton to Darnford. But the signs which warn that the roads are not maintained in winter are a timely reminder that nature is still a force to be reckoned with here.

In the centre of this edition we have used the first edition Ordnance Survey map of about the time of Rev Carr's ordeal to indicate the route which we think he must have followed. Needless to say this is not a route which you should attempt to follow over the hill yourself, even on a clear day in the height of summer. Inevitably, since Carr was hopelessly lost, it does not follow recognised paths and it plunges down some of the steepest slopes on the hill.

We have retained the original spelling of Wolstaston even though the map indicates it was already spelt Woolstaston in the 1860s.

We trust that this edition will help to keep alive a remarkable story by a remarkable character into the 21st century. We would be delighted to hear from any reader who can shed more light on Rev. Carr or earlier editions of his story, for the record in the Local Studies Library is far from complete and our researches have have revealed little about Rev. Carr himself.

Andrew M. Jenkinson,
Bucknell
July 1998

INTRODUCTION

*I*n publishing the following account of "A Night in the Snow," which has been given as a Lecture before the Society for the Promotion of Religious and Useful Knowledge at Bridgnorth, I feel that some apology is due. My preservation through the night of the 29th of January last was doubtless most wonderful, and my experience perhaps almost without precedent, in this country at least; for, though many people have at different times been lost in the snow, scarcely any one has passed through the ordeal of such a day and night as that undergone by myself, and lived to tell the tale. Still I should never have thought that the matter was of sufficient importance to justify me in printing an account of it, had I not discovered that my adventure has created a public interest, for which I was totally unprepared. I have been so repeatedly asked to write a detailed account of all the circumstances connected with my wanderings on the Long Mynd in the snow during that night and the following day, and to have it published, that I have at last (though, I must confess, somewhat reluctantly) consented to do so, and with that view have drawn up the following account.

In writing my story, I have been obliged to go into many very small matters of detail, which may perhaps appear trivial; but it seemed to me that the interest of a story of this kind, if there be any interest attached to it, generally turns upon minor circumstances. I have also been obliged to speak of myself in a very personal manner, but I did not see how I could put the reader in possession of the geographical points of the case, without describing the duties I had to perform, and the country I had to traverse. It only remains for me to add, that should any profits arise from the sale of a "A Night in the Snow", they will be devoted to the restoration of Wolstaston Church now in progress.

E. DONALD CARR. Wolstaston Rectory, April 17, 1865.

A Night in the Snow

*T*he mountains of South-West Shropshire are less known to the lovers of fine scenery than their great beauty deserves, though they are familiar to most geologists as the typical region of the lowest fossil-bearing deposits. Of this group of hills the highest is the Long Mynd, a mountain district of very remarkable character, and many miles in extent. It is about ten miles long, and from three to four miles in breadth. Its summit is a wide expanse of table land, the highest part of which is nearly seventeen hundred feet above the level of the sea. The whole of this unenclosed moorland is covered with gorse and heather, making it extremely gay in the summer time; it is also tolerably abundant in grouse and black game[1], and so fruitful in bilberries, that from £400 to £500 worth are said to have been gathered in the course of a single season. On first hearing it, this sounds an improbable statement; but any one who has been upon the mountain in a good "whinberry season" as it is called, will readily understand that this is no exaggeration. To the poor people of miles around, the "whinberry picking" is the great event of the year. The whole family

Whinberry pickers in the early 1900s photographed by E.S. Cobbold.

betake themselves to the hill with the early morning, carrying with them their provisions for the day; and not unfrequently a kettle to prepare tea forms part of the load. I know no more picturesque sight than that presented by the summit of the Long Mynd towards four o'clock on an August afternoon, when numerous fires are lit amongst the heather, and as many kettles

---

1 *Local tradition has it that red grouse had only been introduced to the Long Mynd in the 1840s. Black game (or black grouse) have become extinct on the hill.*

steaming away on the top of them, while noisy, chattering groups of women and children are clustered round, glad to rest after a hard day's work. A family will pick many quarts of bilberries in the day, and as these are sold at prices varying from 3d. to 5d. a quart, it will be readily understood that it is by no means impossible that the large sum of £400 or £500 should thus be realised in a single season[1].

The appearance of this Long Mynd mountain on the northern side, looking towards Shrewsbury, presents no feature of striking interest, and the ascent is a gradual one, leading chiefly through cultivated ground; but the aspect of the south-eastern or Stretton side is wild in the extreme, the whole face of the mountain being broken up into deep ravines, with precipitous sides, where purple rocks project boldly through the turf, and in many places even the active sheep and

A rugged view of Townbrook Hollow on the east side of the Long Mynd as portrayed in the 1830s by geologist Thomas Wright.

mountain ponies can scarcely find a footing. Down each of these ravines runs a small stream of exquisitely pure water, one of which near the entrance of the valley, becomes considerable enough to turn a mill for carding wool. This stream falls over rocks at the head of the ravine, in a small cascade of a considerable height called the Light Spout.

Many people have lost their lives among these hills at different times, and places here and there bear such suggestive names, as "Dead Man's Beach", "Dead Man's Hollow", etc. The last fair, too, which is held at Church Stretton before Christmas is locally known as "Dead Man's Fair", several men have perished whilst attempting to return home after it across the hill in the dark November night. No one, however, till this winter has been lost for many years. Two drovers were the last persons who perished here, and they lost their lives near a place called "The Thresholds", in a deep snow which fell in April thirty-seven years ago.

---

1 *Bilberry picking remained a significant part of the local economy until the Second World War; but today, though bilberry still flourishes, it is difficult to find enough fruit for a decent pie!*

The western slope of the Long Mynd is less strikingly picturesque and more desolate, but the view from the top in this direction is the finest of any. Almost unseen in a narrow valley at the foot of the mountain, stand the village and church of Ratlinghope, the centre of a parish numbering about three hundred souls only, but which stretches over miles of mountain country, embracing a portion of the wild mining district of the Stiper Stones. Beyond these hills the eye passes to the Welsh mountains, and rests at last on the grand peaks of Cader Idris in one direction, and Snowdon in the other, which may be seen in clear weather sharply defined against a sun-set sky.

Poor Ratlinghope was in sore need of some one to look after it when the living was offered to me in September 1856. It had at that time been left for many Sundays together without service, the late incumbent residing in Shrewsbury, twelve miles distant, and being frequently prevented by ill health from coming over. There is no house in the parish where a clergyman can live, or even procure tolerable lodgings; and if there were, there is next to nothing, as one of the parishioners said to me the other day, "to find coals to warm it with." It is scarcely to be wondered at that under these circumstances, when the living became vacant in the summer of 1856, there was no suitable person to be found who was willing to accept so desirable a piece of preferment. The parish of Wolstaston, of which I have the charge, and in which I reside, is situated on high ground on the eastern slope of the Long Mynd, i.e. exactly on the opposite side of the mountain to Ratlinghope. Above Wolstaston the ground rises steadily for about a mile and a half till you come to the unenclosed moorland, which stretches away for many miles of open country, covered with heather and gorse. It was under the circumstances that I have already mentioned that the living of

8

Ratlinghope was offered to me. I was aware that it would be impossible to attend to the parish as one would wish to do, with four miles of the wild hill country to cross between the two villages. Still, as no one else could be found to take it, and I thought that the Ratlinghope people might think that "half-a-loaf was better than no bread," I consented to accept the living, and to do the best I could from three o'clock in the afternoon to six, which enabled me to give an afternoon service at Ratlinghope every Sunday[1].

I soon found, however, that the task I had undertaken was no very light one, as the only access from Wolstaston to Ratlinghope was by mountain tracks, over the highest part of the Long Mynd, unless indeed one drove round the base of the hill, a distance of at least twelve miles. The ride was pleasant enough in fine weather, but less enjoyable when fogs hung heavy over the hill, when the tracks were slippery with ice, or when falling snow concealed every landmark. It not unfrequently happened in winter, when the snow was very deep, or much drifted, that it was impossible to ride across the hill, and the expedition then had to be performed on foot; still I always managed to cross somehow in spite of wind or weather, so that during the last eight years and a half the little mountain church has never been without one Sunday service. I find that during that time I have crossed the Long Mynd (in round numbers) nearly two thousand five hundred times; consequently my knowledge of the country became so intimate, that I felt equally at home upon the hill in all weathers, and at all hours of the day and night. On one occasion, I had to cross it late on a November night and in a dense fog, when returning home from Ratlinghope, and met with no accident; and I think that this and similar experiences made me somewhat over confident. I mention this to show how little the most perfect acquaintance with country will avail any one when overtaken by such a blinding snow storm as that of the 29th of January last.

During the preceding week the snow fell heavily, and accumulated on the hills to a greater depth than had been known for fifty-one years. Public

---

1 *Clearly the problems of staffing rural parishes are nothing new. However, today Wolstaston is grouped with Dorrington, Leebotwood, Longnor and Stapleton to the north of the Long Mynd; Ratlinghope with Wentnor, Norbury, Myndtown and other parishes to the west.*

opinion was unanimous that there had been nothing like it since 1814. A strong wind, moreover, had so drifted it that the roads were impassable, and the communication between neighbouring villages, and even between houses in the same village, almost ceased. Letters wont to be received in the morning arrived late in the day, or not at all; and unhappy folk who were unprovided with a good store of food or coals had either to borrow of their neighbours or starve. The morning service at Wolstaston on Sunday the 29th was of necessity but thinly attended, and it seemed probable that I should not even be expected at Ratlinghope. As, however, the service there had never been omitted owing to bad weather, I was anxious to get to my little church if possible; in fact, I considered it my duty to make the attempt, though I felt very doubtful whether I should succeed.

Accordingly, very soon after morning service at Wolstaston was over, I started on the expedition. I was in such a hurry to be off that I could not stay to take my usual luncheon, but swallowed a few mouthfuls of soup, and put a small flask containing about three ounces of brandy in my pocket. My taking anything of the kind with me was a most unprecedented circumstance. I only remember one other occasion in which I did so, and that was also in a very deep snow; but now foreseeing a walk of no common difficulty, I thought the precaution a wise one, and saw reason afterwards to be thankful that I had adopted it.

I started on horseback, though I knew that I could only ride a short distance, but thought it advisable to save myself all unnecessary fatigue. I was of course accompanied by a servant to bring back the horses when they were of no further use. By leaving the lane and making our way across the fields over hedge and ditch, we contrived to ride about half a mile. The horses then became useless, as the drifts were so deep against the hedges and gates, that the poor animals became imbedded in them, and were unable to find any firm footing to leap from. The servant therefore had to return with them long before I reached the unenclosed mountain land, and I proceeded on my way alone.

The journey proved more difficult even than I had expected. The snow was for the most part up to the knees and very soft, and the drifts were so deep that they could only be crossed by crawling on hands and knees, as any one will readily understand who has attempted to cross deep snow when in a soft state. When I reached the open moorland the day was bright and fine, and the snow stretched around me for miles in a dazzling expanse very painful to the eyes, and unbroken by track, landmark, or footprint of any living creature. The form of the country, however, was a sufficient guide to my destination, and after a severe struggle over and through the drifts, I reached my little church at a quarter-past three o'clock, just two hours and a quarter from the time I had left Wolstaston. A few people were assembled together, though no one had really expected me, and after a short service I started on my homeward journey, having refused the invitations of my kind people to stay the night amongst them, as I was anxious to get back to Wolstaston in time for my six o'clock evening service, and I did not anticipate that I should encounter any greater difficulties in my return home than I had done in coming to Ratlinghope.

During the three quarters of an hour, however, that we had been in church, the aspect of the weather had completely changed. A furious gale had come on from E.S.E., which, as soon as I got on the open moorland, I found was driving clouds of snow and icy sleet before it. It was with considerable difficulty that I made my way up the western ascent of the hill, as I had to walk in the teeth of this gale. The force of the wind was most extraordinary. I have been in many furious gales, but never in anything to compare with that, as it took me off my legs, and blew me flat down upon the ground over and over again. The sleet too was most painful, stinging one's face, and causing such injury to the eyes, that it was impossible to lift up one's head. I contrived, however, to fight my way through it, and at length reached the crest of the hill. Though I could not see many yards in any direction, I knew at this time exactly where I was, as I passed the carcase of a mountain pony which I had previously noticed. The poor thing had no doubt been famished to death, and was fast wasting to a skeleton. Numbers of these hardy little animals have perished during the severe weather from hunger, having been previously reduced to the lowest condition through lack of pasturage during the dry season of 1864. One man, who owned fourteen of them, has lost every one.

Leaving this solitary waymark, the half buried skeleton, by which I had rested for a few minutes and taken a little of my brandy, I started again, having first made a careful observation of the direction in which I should go. After a further struggle across the level summit of the hill, I reached my second landmark, a pool in a little hollow between the hills[1], which is well known to the inhabitants of the district, and interesting to naturalists, as the resort of curlews and other rare birds; here again I took a short rest and then started upon what I fondly dreamed would be the last difficult stage of my journey.

My way from the pool lay first up a steep ascent for rather less than half a mile to the top of the hill, and then across a level flat for some three or four hundred yards, when a fir plantation would be reached at the edge of the enclosed ground.[2] Once within the friendly shelter of those firs, I knew that the remainder of my walk, though still tedious and fatiguing, would be comparatively easy. It pleased God, however, that I should never reach them that night. Doubtless I had been too confident in my own powers, and at the very time when I thought the difficulties and dangers of my task were well nigh accomplished, I was taught a lesson which I shall remember to the latest hour of my life. I ascended the hill to the flat already spoken of, though it was a very slow process, for owing to the depth of the drifts, which were now increasing rapidly, and the force of the wind, I was compelled to crawl a great part of the way. The storm now came on, if possible, with increased fury. It was quite impossible to look up or see for a yard around, and the snow came down so thick and fast that my servant, who had come some distance up the lane from Wolstaston in hopes of seeing something of me, describing it to me afterwards, said, "Sir, it was just as if they were throwing it on to us out of buckets." I fought on through it, however, expecting soon to come to the fir wood. On and on I went, but not a glimpse of its friendly shelter could I see, the real fact being that I had bourne away a great deal too much to the right,

---

1 *Presumably a pre-cursor of the Wildmoor pools, but not shown on the map of the time. The present series of pools created by damming the stream is said to date from the 1940s.*

2 *This fir plantation is probably the one shown south west of High Park House which has all but disappeared again. The present plantation to the north of the road is much more recent.*

almost at right angles to my proper course. Having been blown down over and over again, I had probably, in rising to my feet, altered my direction unconsciously. The wind too, by which I had been trying to steer, proved a treacherous compass; for, as I have been told, about this time it went more round into the south. It was, moreover, becoming very dark. After a while I became aware that the ground under my feet was of a wrong shape, sloping downwards when it should have been level, and I then knew that I had missed my way. This, however, gave me no great uneasiness, as I imagined that I had only gone a little too much to the south of the wood, and that I should soon reach an inhabited district at the bottom of it, known as Bullock's Moor, from which a somewhat circuitous route would bring me safely home. Under this impression I walked cheerfully on, but only for a few steps further. Suddenly my feet flew from under me, and I found myself shooting at a fearful pace down the side of one of the steep ravines which I had imagined lay far away to my right. I thought to check myself by putting my stick behind me, and bearing heavily upon it in the manner usual under such circumstances in Alpine travelling. Before, however, I could do so I came in contact with something which jerked it out of my hand and turned me round, so that I continued my tremendous glissade head downwards, lying on my back.

The pace I was going in this headlong descent must have been very great, yet it seemed to me to occupy a marvellous  space of time, long enough for the events of my whole previous life to pass in review before me, as I had often before heard that they did in moments of extreme peril. I never lost my consciousness, but had time to think much of those I should leave behind me, expecting every moment as I did to be dashed over the rocks at the bottom of the ravine; for I knew in fact that such must be my fate, unless

I could stop myself by some means. Owing to the softness of the snow, I contrived to accomplish this by kicking my foot as deep into the snow as I could, and at the same time bending my knee with a smart muscular effort, so as to make a hook of my leg; this brought me to a stand still, but my position was anything but agreeable even then, hanging head downwards on a very steep part, and never knowing any moment but what I might start again. With much difficulty, however, I at length succeeded in getting myself the right way up, and then descended with great care to the bottom of the ravine, intending if possible to walk along the course of the stream in its hollow till it should lead me to the enclosed country. The ravine, however, was so choked up with snow, that to walk along the valley was utterly impossible. The drifts were many feet over my head, in several places they must have been at least twenty feet in depth; and having once got into them, I had the greatest difficulty, by scratching and struggling, to extricate myself from them again. It was now dark. I did not know into which of the ravines I had fallen, for at this part there is a complete network of them intersecting each other in every direction. The only way by which I had thought to escape was hopelessly blocked up, and I had to face the awful fact that I was lost among the hills, should have to spend the night there, and that, humanly speaking, it was almost impossible that I could survive it.

The instinct of self-preservation, however, is strong, even when a fearful death seems close at hand, and there were others for whose sake, even more than my own, I desired that night that my life might be spared, if such were God's will. I knew that, under Providence, all depended on my own powers of endurance, and that the struggle for life must be a very severe one. The depth of the snow made walking a very exhausting effort. It was always up to my knees, more often up to my waist; but my only chance, as I was well aware, was to keep moving; and having extricated myself at last from the drifts in the ravine, I began to climb the opposite side of the hill, though I had not the least idea in which direction I ought to go. As I made my way upwards, I saw just in front of me what looked like a small shadow flitting about, for owing to the white ground it was never completely dark. I was much surprised at this, especially as when I came to it, it disappeared into the snow, with the exception of one round dark spot, which remained motionless. I put my hand down upon this dark object to ascertain what it could possibly be, and found that I had got hold of a hare's head! I saw many of these little animals in the course of the night.[1] They made holes in the snow for shelter, and sat in them well protected by their warm coats, happier far than their human fellow-sufferer, who knew that for him there must be no rest that night if he would see the light of another day.

Having climbed the hill, I walked along its crest for some distance, till suddenly I again lost my footing, and shot down the hill, as far as I can judge, on the opposite side into another ravine. This was, if possible, a more fearful glissade than my previous one; it was a very precipitous place, and I was whirled round and round in my descent, sometimes head first, sometimes feet first, and again sideways, rolling over and over, till at last, by clutching at the gorse bushes, and digging my feet into the snow as before, I once more managed to check my wild career, and bring myself to a stand; but I had lost my hat and a pair of warm fur gloves, which I had on over a pair of old dogskins. The loss of these fur gloves proved very serious to me, as my hands soon began to get so numbed with the cold, that they were comparatively useless. At the bottom of the ravine into which I had now fallen, I found myself again involved in snow drifts, and had still more difficulty than before in getting out of them. I had tumbled into a very soft one far over my head, and had to fight, and scratch, and burrow for a long time before I could extricate myself, and became more exhausted than at any other time during the night. I only ventured to take my brandy very sparingly, wishing to husband it as much as possible, and there was but a very tiny drop left. My hands, as I have said, were so numbed with cold as to be nearly useless. I had the greatest difficulty in holding the flask, or in eating snow for refreshment, and could hardly get my hands to my mouth for the masses of ice which had formed

---

1 *Hares are a rare sight today on the Long Mynd, though rabbits are plentiful at most times.*

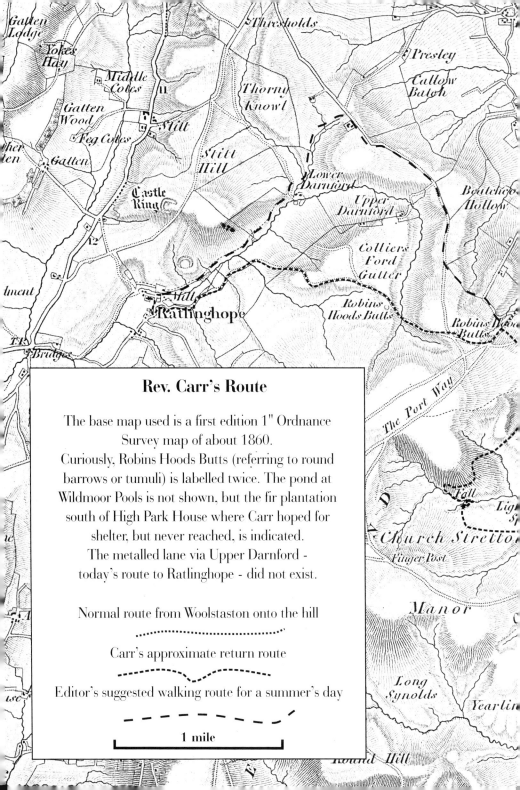

Gatten Lodge
Yokes Hay
Thresholds
Presley
Middle Cotes
Callow Batch
Thorny Knowl
Gatten Wood
Stitt
Feg Cotes
Gatten
Stitt Hill
Lower Darnford
Upper Darnford
Beatchco Hollow
Castle Ring
Colliers Ford Gutter
Mill
Ratlinghope
Robins Hoods Butts
Robins Hood Butts
Bridges
The Port Way
Fall
Lig St
Church Strettor
Finger Post
Manor
Long Synolds
Yearlin
Round Hill

Rev. Carr's Route

The base map used is a first edition 1" Ordnance Survey map of about 1860.

Curiously, Robins Hoods Butts (referring to round barrows or tumuli) is labelled twice. The pond at Wildmoor Pools is not shown, but the fir plantation south of High Park House where Carr hoped for shelter, but never reached, is indicated.

The metalled lane via Upper Darnford - today's route to Ratlinghope - did not exist.

Normal route from Woolstaston onto the hill

Carr's approximate return route

Editor's suggested walking route for a summer's day

1 mile

Tumulus

Parsonage

Old Wind Mills 9

Leasowes

Night Shell

Castle hill

Station

Batches

Le Botwood

Tumulus

Woolstaston

Hollyhurst

Station

Greenway Cottage

Lower Wood

Collier's Ley

Brook House 10

Watling Street

Holly Hurst

Park House

Womerton

Pennsylvania

Dudgley

Inwood

Bullock's Moor

Quaking Brook Bridge

Dudgley Cottage

Young Oak Coppice

Caer

Lady Ley

Whorsley

Botvyle

Little Caradoc

Synold's Coppice

Mill Brick Field

Caradoc

Caer Caradoc

Batch

Houghton Coppice

Caer Hill

All Stretton

Bodbury Ring

Cwmdoytch 12

Caradoc Coppice

Carding Mill

Battle Monument

Devils Mouth

Mill Glen

New Farm

Cwm

Hope Bowdler Hill

Burway

Ash Brook

Helmeth Hill

Dingle

Station

Gaerstone Rock

The Rectory

Battle Field

CHURCH STRETTON 13

Hopes Wood

World's End 15

Harley

T.P.

Hope-batch Dingle

Way

Harley Hill

Wood

Brockhurst Castle

Coles Wood

upon my whiskers, and which were gradually developed into a long crystal beard, hanging halfway to my waist. Icicles likewise had formed about my eyes and eyebrows, which I frequently had to break off, and my hair had frozen into a solid block of ice. After the loss of my hat, my hair must, I suppose, have become filled with snow, while I was overhead in the drifts. Probably this was partially melted by the warmth of my head, and subsequently converted to ice by the intense frost. Large balls of ice also formed upon my cuffs, and underneath my knees, which encumbered me very much in walking, and I had continually to break them off. I tried to supply the place of my hat by tying my handkerchief over my head, but found that by no possible effort could I make a knot, and that I could only keep it on my head by holding the corners between my teeth. It was equally impossible to refasten my overcoat, only a thin tweed (for I had dressed lightly, in expectation of hard exercise), which had become unbuttoned in my last fall. It may seem absurd to mention it, but the cravings of hunger grew so keen, stimulated as they were by the cold and the great exertion, that it actually occurred to me whether I could eat one of my dogskin gloves. I was, however, deterred from making the attempt, partly by the prospect of its toughness, and partly by fear of greater injury to my hands from frost bite, if they were deprived of their last covering. My exhaustion was so great that I fell down every two or three steps, and the temptation to give in and lie down in the snow became almost irresistible, and had to be struggled against with every power of mind and body. I endeavoured to keep constantly before me the certain fact, that if sleep once overcame me I should never wake again in this life. The night seemed interminably long. Again and again I tried to calculate the time, but always came to the same conclusion, that many hours must elapse before the return of daylight. The wind had gone down, and the stillness became so oppressive, that I often spoke aloud for the sake of hearing my own voice, and to ascertain that the cold, which was intense, had not deprived me of the power of speech. The hares still sported and burrowed on the hill sides, but excepting these there were no signs of life whatever.

Never did a shipwrecked mariner watch for the morning more anxiously than did I through that weary, endless night, for I knew that a glimpse of the distance in any one direction would enable me to steer my course homewards. Day dawned at last, but hope and patience were to be yet further tried, for a dense fog clung to the face of the hill, obscuring everything but the objects close at hand. Furthermore, I discovered that I was rapidly becoming snow blind. My eyes, which had been considerably injured already by the sharp sleet of the evening before, were further affected by the glare of the snow, and I was fast losing all distinctness of vision. I first learned the extent of this new calamity when endeavouring, with the earliest light, to look at my watch. It was a work of great difficulty to get it out of my pocket; and when this was done, I found that I could not tell the face from the back. The whole thing was hazy and indistinct, and I can only describe it as looking like an orange seen through a mist. Such sight as remained rapidly became all confusion as regards the form, colour, and proportion of objects. Again and again I thought I saw before me trees and enclosures, but these, when I came up to them, invariably turned out to be only portions of gorse bushes projecting through the snow. My optical delusions as to COLOUR were perhaps the most remarkable; the protruding rocks invariably appeared of a strange orange yellow, with black lines along them, producing a sort of tortoise-shell effect. I took these mysterious appearances at first for dead animals, ponies or sheep, and touched them to try to ascertain the fact. My hands, however, were so utterly devoid of sensation, that they were of no more use than my eyes in identifying objects. I was therefore quite in the dark as to their nature, till experience proved them to be rocks with tufts of heather on them. Owing to my failing eyesight, my falls became very frequent, and several of them were from heights so great that it would scarcely be believed were I to attempt to describe them. I may, however, say that they were such as perfectly to appall those who, a few days afterwards, visited the spots where they occurred, and saw the deep impressions in the snow where I had plunged into it from the rocks above. One fall especially I well remember. I had just crossed the ridge of a hill, and saw, as I imagined, close below me a pool covered with ice, which seemed free from snow. I thought I would walk across this, and, accordingly, made a slight jump from the rock on which I stood in order to reach it. In a moment, however, I discovered that, instead of on to a pool, I had jumped into empty space. I must have fallen on this occasion a considerable distance, but I was caught in a deep snow drift, so that, although considerably shaken and bewildered for the moment by what had happened, I was not seriously hurt.

I have been enabled by various circumstances, and by the help of those who followed my tracks before the snow melted, to make out with tolerable accuracy the course of my wanderings. Those who tracked me say that, "If there was one part of the hill more difficult and dangerous than another, that is the line which Mr. Carr took."

When the morning light first dawned, I could see that I was walking along the side of a ravine of great depth, and more than usually perpendicular sides; it was so steep that I could not climb to the top of the ridge and get out of it, and the snow was in such a very loose, soft state, that I expected every moment it would give way beneath me, and I should be precipitated into the depths below. I had to walk with the greatest care to prevent this; and I believe that this was a very good thing for me, as it gave my mind complete occupation, and kept me from flagging. I could only go straight on, as I could not ascend, and was afraid to descend. My method of progression was more crawling than walking, as I had to drive my hands deep into the snow, and clutch at tufts of grass or heather, or any thing I could find beneath it, to hold on by. I must have gone forward in this way for an hour or two, when I found the ravine becoming less steep, and I heard the sound of running water very distinctly. Accordingly I thought I would descend and try once more whether I could walk down the stream, as this by its sound seemed a larger one, and I thought It might have cut a way through the drifts. I reached the bottom of the valley safely. It appears to have been the valley immediately above the Light Spout waterfall, and, trying to walk by the stream, I tumbled over the first upper fall. Hearing a noise of falling water, and seeing dimly rocks all round me, I found it would not do to go forward in this direction, so, having unconsciously gone to the very edge of the lower cascade, where I must in all probability have been killed had I fallen over, I turned sharply up the hill again by a very steep place. Round and round this waterfall I seemed to have climbed in every possible direction. A man who had tracked me, and with whom I visited the place a few weeks ago, said, "You seem to have had a deal o' work to do here, Sir," pointing to a small rocky space at the bottom of the fall. I had imagined, while thus going round and round as if on a tread mill, that I was walking straight forward down stream, and I suppose my efforts to keep near the sound of the water misled me. Though perfectly familiar with this part of the Long Mynd, I was so blind at this time, and everything looked so strange, that I did not in the least recognise my position. Finding I did not get on very well, I determined now to try whether I could walk or crawl down the actual stream itself where it had hollowed its way underneath the drifts which overhung it, making a sort of low-arched tunnel, which I thought worth trying. I soon found, however, that this was quite impracticable, and that if I went on I should either be suffocated or hopelessly imbedded in the snow, and that then my utmost efforts would fail to extricate me. It also occurred to me somewhat painfully, that if I lost my life, as I thought I inevitably must do now, my body would not be found for days, or it might be weeks, if it were buried deep in the mountain of snow at the bottom of that valley; and I was anxious that what remained of me might be found soon, and that the dreadful suspense, which is worse than the most fearful certainty, might thus be spared to all those who cared about my fate.

I was not, however, quite beat yet; so, retracing my steps, I determined once more to leave the stream and make for the higher ground. But a new misfortune now befell me: I lost my boots. They were strong laced boots, without elastic sides, or any such weak points about them. I had observed before that one was getting loose, but was unable to do anything to it from the numbness of my hands; and after struggling out of a deep drift previous to reascending the hill, I found that I had left this boot behind. There was nothing for it but to go on without, and as my feet were perfectly numbed from the cold, and devoid of feeling, I did not experience any difficulty or pain on this account. That boot was afterwards found on a ledge of rock near the waterfall. I soon after lost the other one, or rather, I should say, it came off, and I could not get it on again, so I carried it in my hand some time, but lost it in one of my many severe falls. The fact of the loss of my boots has astonished all those who have heard of it, and I believe has excited more comment than any other part of my adventure. I have even heard of its being a matter of fierce dispute, on more than one occasion, whether laced bouts COULD come off in this way. They do not seem to have become unlaced, as the laces were firmly knotted, but had burst in the middle, and the whole front of the boot had been stretched out of shape from the strain put upon it whilst laboriously dragging my feet out of deep drifts for so many hours together, which I can only describe as acting upon the boots like a steam-power boot-jack[1].

And so for hours I walked on in my stockings without inconvenience. Even when I trod upon gorse bushes, I did not feel it, as my feet had become as insensible as my hands. It had occurred to me now that I might be in the Carding Mill valley, and that I would steer my course on that supposition. It was fortunate that I did so, for I was beginning to think that I could not now hold out much longer, and was struggling in a part where the drifts were up nearly to my neck, when I heard what I had thought never to hear again – the blessed sound of human voices, children's voices, talking and laughing, and apparently sliding not very far off. I called to them with all my might, but judge of my dismay when sudden and total silence took the place of the merry voices I had so lately heard! I shouted again and again, and said that I was lost, but there was no reply. It was a bitter disappointment, something like that of the sailor shipwrecked on a desert island, who sees a sail approaching and thinks that he is saved, when as he gazes the vessel shifts her course and disappears on the horizon, dashing his hopes to the ground. It appeared, as I learned afterwards, that these children saw ME, though I could not see them, and ran away terrified at my unearthly aspect. Doubtless the head of a man protruding from a deep snow drift, crowned and bearded with ice like a ghastly emblem of winter, was a sight to cause a panic among children, and one cannot wonder that they ran off to communicate the news that "there was the bogie in the snow." Happily, however, for the bogie, he had noticed the direction from which these voices came, and struggling forward again, I soon found myself sufficiently near to the Carding Mill to

---

1 *The fate of the boots is discussed in the postscript on page 32.*

recognise the place, blind as I was. A little girl now ventured to approach me, as, true to the instincts of her nature, the idea dawned upon her that I was no goblin of the mountains, no disagreeable thing from a world beneath popped up through the snow, but a real fellow-creature in distress. I spoke to her and told her that I was the clergyman of Ratlinghope, and had been lost in the snow on the hill all night. As she did not answer at once, I suppose she was taking a careful observation of me, for after a few moments she said "Why, you look like Mr. Carr of Wolstaston." "I am Mr. Carr," I replied; whereupon the boys, who had previously run away, and, as I imagine, taken refuge behind the girl, came forward and helped me on to the little hamlet, only a few yards distant, where some half dozen cottages are clustered together round the Carding Mill.

The Carding Mill and cottages pictured in a rare early photograph of about 1860

I was saved, at any rate, from immediate peril, though I fully expected that serious illness must follow from my violent exertions and long exposure. I was saved at all events from the death of lonely horror against which I had wrestled so many hours in mortal conflict, and scarcely knew how to believe that I was once more among my fellow-men, under a kindly, hospitable roof.

God's hand had led me thither. No wisdom or power of my own could have availed for my deliverance, when once my sight was so much gone. The Good Shepherd had literally, in very deed, led the blind by a way that he knew not to a refuge of safety and peace.

The good kind people at the Carding Mill, you may be sure, soon gathered round me in sympathising wonder, and I was quickly supplied with such comforts as they could give. I told them that I had had scarcely anything to eat since breakfast the day before (as I had been too much hurried to eat my luncheon before starting to Ratlinghope), and so tea and bread and butter were at once provided. For the former I was very grateful, But I could hardly eat the latter, as all feeling of hunger had left me. The good people were much shocked to find that I could not pick up a piece of bread and butter for myself, as I could neither feel it nor see it; I believe they thought my sight was hopelessly gone. I was, however, under no uneasiness myself on this score, as I was perfectly familiar with snow blindness, having seen cases of it in Switzerland, and knew that in all probability my eyes would get quite right again in a week's time, as it turned out that they did. They also discovered that the middle finger of my right hand was terribly lacerated, and that the skin was completely stripped off the back of it. This I knew to be a much more serious affair, as the frost had evidently got fast hold of it, and I thought it very likely that I should lose it. This, however, seemed a very trifling matter to me then. Had it been my right arm I should have thought nothing of it, after so marvellous an escape. I was provided at the Carding Mill with a hat, boots, and dry stockings; and having rested about a quarter of an hour, set out again to Church Stretton, about a mile distant. A man from the cottage came with me, and gave me his arm, and with this assistance I accomplished the walk with comparative ease. I was so anxious to get home, that I almost felt as if I could have walked the whole way, though I do not suppose that I could really have done so, my home being rather more than five miles off. Arrived at the town, I sent my companion for medical assistance, and myself made my way to the Crown Inn[1]. I could discern large objects sufficiently to

---

1 *Subsequently rebuilt and known as The Hotel, and currently The Old Coppers Malt House*

find my way along the street, though all was blurred and indistinct, and the admission of light to my eyes was beginning to cause me extreme pain. I ordered a fly immediately to take me as far as possible on my road home. No vehicle of any description had been along the turnpike road that day, and it was very doubtful how far a fly could go, so it was arranged that we should be accompanied by a man on a saddle horse, that I might ride when the fly could go no further, as I knew that, under the most favourable circumstances, the last mile and a half of the road to Wolstaston would be inaccessible to wheels.

Of course my adventure excited great interest at the Crown Hotel, when it was fully understood what had happened to me. It was just two o'clock in the afternoon when I reached that place, and as I had left Ratlinghope at four o'clock on the previous afternoon, I had been walking uninterruptedly for twenty-two hours, excepting the quarter of an hour I had rested at the Carding Mill. My good friends at the hotel discovered that my clothes were very wet, for they had been frozen before and were now thawed, so I was dressed up in the landlord's garments. The effect must have been very ludicrous, for he was a much stouter man than I was at any time, and now I had shrunk away to nothing. It will not therefore be wondered at that people when they saw me declared they should not have known who I was.

The surgeon having come and dressed my finger, and warned me to keep away from fire and hot water, and having prescribed some hot brandy and water, I started in my fly on my homeward journey. Very slow was our progress. We had taken spades with us, and many times the driver and the man who accompanied him had to dig a way for the fly to get through. Most trying was the long delay thus caused to a man who knew that in his own home he must probably be reckoned among the dead; but there was no help for it, and at last Leebotwood was reached, the place where the lane to Wolstaston turned off from the main road, and where I was to leave the fly, and, as I hoped, ride home.

The Post Office is at Leebotwood, and having given orders there that any letters coming from my house should be stopped, I was helped on my horse, and, accompanied by the man, began to ascend the hill. I had not gone a hundred yards, when it became evident that it would be impossible to ride far, and that I should be obliged to walk again, so the horse was sent back to Leebotwood by a man whom we met, and I started again on my own feet. Just at this time we met another man coming down over the fields from Wolstaston. He had letters with him to post; those letters were from my home. They were to say that I had been lost in the snow storm, that every effort had been made to find me, that they had proved fruitless, and that there was no hope left. I sent the messenger back again pretty quickly, and told him to go home as fast as he could and say I was coming. This news reached the village about half an hour before I could get up there myself, and as may be supposed there was great rejoicing. So completely had all hope of my safety been given up, that to my people it seemed almost like a resurrection from the dead.

They had made the greatest efforts to find me. Twice a party had gone up the hill on the Sunday night to the limit of the enclosed ground, and stayed there calling and shouting, till, as one of them said to me, they felt that if they had stayed there another ten minutes, they would have been frozen to death. The second time they went up that night, they actually got on to the open moorland some two or three hundred yards, but here they were in imminent danger of being lost themselves. One of them indeed declared that he could not return, and would have been lost had not his companions insisted on his struggling back with them. Human effort could do no more, and they made their toilsome way home prostrated with fatigue.

It was a fearful moment, they tell me, when the Rectory house was closed up for the night, the shutters fastened, and curtains drawn, with the fate of its master unknown. The helpless watchers could only wait and count the weary hours, keeping food hot for the wanderer, who they feared would never return, and unable till the morning to plan any further efforts for his rescue. The awful wind raged on, sometimes assuming to the ears of the excited listeners the sound of rolling wheels and horses' feet, startling them into expectation, though they knew that the tramp of an army would have fallen noiseless on that depth of snow. Then again, it rose like shrieks and wild calls of distress, and every now and then would smite the house with a buffet, as though it would level it with the ground.

The storm lulled at length, as the hours went slowly by. Morning came and the men prepared to resume their almost hopeless search once more. They started, about twenty strong, armed with spades and shovels, and determined first of all to cut their way to Ratlinghope, thinking that perhaps I had remained there all night. They worked with all their might, but the snow was deeper than ever, and their progress was laborious and very slow. Though they had started as soon as it was light in the morning, they did not reach Ratlinghope till noon, and then their last hope was dashed to the ground, for they heard that I HAD started the previous afternoon, though pressed to remain in the village for the night. Great was the consternation of the Ratlinghope people when they heard the news. They knew the hill well, and said with one consent, "If Mr. Carr was on the Long Mynd last night, he is a dead man." This conviction too was strengthened by the sad fact, that that very morning the dead body of a man, whom we all knew well, had been found in the road frozen to death, not more than one hundred and fifty yards from a small hamlet in the parish of Ratlinghope, known as "The Bridges". Poor Easthope, for such was his name, was a journeyman shoemaker by trade. He owned a few ponies which were on the hill, and he had been looking after these on the Sunday. I suppose he was much exhausted by this, but he had safely reached his daughter's house in the evening, which he subsequently left to go to the place where he worked, no great distance off. He was found, as I have said, the next morning frozen to death on the turnpike road. It is conjectured that he either sat down to rest or fell down, and that he speedily became insensible. I think this fact in itself is sufficient to prove that, had I given way to the temptation to rest, I too should have lost my life.

The searching party, reinforced by most of the able-bodied men in Ratlinghope, beat that part of the hill lying between Ratlinghope and Wolstaston thoroughly, thinking that I must be somewhere in the tract between the two places, never supposing that I could have wandered as far away as I actually had done. The fog was so thick that it was only by keeping near each other and shouting constantly that this party was able to keep together. I need not say that they failed to discover any trace of me, and about three o'clock in the afternoon, worn out and exhausted, they returned to the

Rectory with the worst tidings. "He must be dead," they said, "he must BE dead; it is not possible that any human creature could have lived through such a night." And it was upon the receipt of these tidings that the letters were sent off which I so fortunately succeeded in stopping. Half an hour after, the news came that I was returning, and in another half-hour I was at home. This was between four and five o'clock in the afternoon, rather more than twenty-seven hours from the time I had left Wolstaston.

I was glad to go to bed at once, and to have my feet and hands well rubbed with snow. This, it should be well known, is the only thing to be done in cases of frost bite. Had I put them in hot water, I should in all probability have lost my fingers and toes; they would have sloughed off. I know several cases where this has happened; indeed, I heard of one quite lately, for the gardener of a friend of mine in Warwickshire had his hands frost bitten while throwing the snow off the roof of a house during this last winter, and injudiciously putting them into hot water, the result has been that he has lost the ends of all his fingers, to the first joint. In my case, I am thankful to say I knew better than to do this, and by the use of cold water and continued friction have succeeded in restoring my hands in a great measure. They have still not nearly as much sensation in them as before, but this will return with time. During the last few weeks, gorse pricks have been working out of my hands and feet and legs by the hundreds, though at first, from the numbness of the skin, I was quite unconscious of them. It is not to be wondered at that I should have picked these up in great numbers whilst walking through the gorse bushes without my boots, and clutching at them as I fell in hopes of saving myself.

Such are the details of my "Night in the Snow," and my most wonderful preservation through it and the following day. I trust that no one who may chance to read these pages will ever be placed in a similar position; but should it so happen, I hope that the remembrance of my adventure will occur to them; for surely it teaches, as plainly as anything can, that even in the most adverse circumstances no one need ever despair; and shows how an individual of no unusual physical powers may, by God's help, resist the overwhelming temptation to sleep which is usually so fatal to those who are lost in the snow.

THE SNOW STORM OF 1865

I have not thought it necessary in these memoranda to give any detailed account of my adventure in the snow storm which occurred on the 29th and 30th of January, 1865, because a tolerably full history of that adventure has been given in my little book " A Night in the Snow," and other particulars are mentioned in a manuscript account of those terrible days written immediately after by my wife. I wish, however, to leave it on record that the account of the storm in the little book is somewhat understated, as I was warned at the time of its publication that if I described the height of the snow drifts and the actual depth of the snow fall as it really occurred, it would never be believed, and that it would throw discredit on the whole story. In deference to that opinion, the account given in the book was considerably modified from its original form as a lecture given at Bridgnorth. It is, however, a fact that when the search party started on the evening of the 29th to try and find me, one of them (our workman, Thomas Hughes) mounted on a large waggon horse rode first to endeavour to force open a track by breaking through the drifts, but in the first big one just above the village he and his horse were completely buried, so that only the crown of his hat (a tall Sunday one) could be seen. On the turnpike road all trace of the turnpike gate which then existed near Leebotwood, had vanished, though there were no specially big drifts there, and in a little cottage farm house on the edge of the hill close to Ratlinghope and just above it (Kite's) it was about 10 days or a fortnight before the inhabitants even heard of my adventure, so blocked up and covered over was the place, that they only just continued to dig out a road to their cowhouse, and so like many others probably, the garrison being fully provisioned, they remained utterly shut off from the outer world till the thaw came. The snow had been falling heavily for some days before the 29th and had already accumulated to a great depth, so that roads had to be cut through the village to enable us to get about at all and when the great fall of the 29th and 30th came in addition to this, it can easily be imagined what a depth it must have become. That snow storm will long be remembered in these parts, for all are agreed that there had been nothing like it for 50 years, "not since the year of the peace" the old people said.

As soon as I was sufficiently recovered from the effects of the exposure and the frost bite etc., to be able to undertake it, we had a special Thanksgiving Service to which we summoned all the search party as well as the parishioners: it was largely attended. It took place on February 10th. The special Psalms selected were XXIII, CIII and CXXI: the Lessons were, first, Isaiah XXV, and second, II Corinthians I. Afterwards all the search party, about 30, had dinner here.

1887 or 1888   E. DONALD CARR.

Postscripts – I: The Boots

Rev Carr makes much of the loss of his boots which he claims burst asunder through the repeated downward pressure. He also refers to their recovery later when retracing his route. In the reserve collection of the Shrewsbury Museum Service, but rarely on display, is a pair of boots which are reputedly the ones worn by Carr during his 'night in the snow'. Clearly they must have been extensively repaired if this is so; for the boots show remarkably little sign of involvement in this adventure. They are without laces, which Carr said remained in tact, and are not split as described. However, they do show a marked change in colour between the brown leather of the top part and the black of the lower section. And the undersides are quite worn with some missing studs.

Did Carr feel such an attachment to these boots that he had them repaired and continued to wear them afterwards, loosing the laces at a later date? We may never know for certain, but if they are authentic (as we have no particular reason to doubt) they are the only tangible relic of this tale.

II: Walking the Long Mynd today

All the open moorland of the Long Mynd across which Carr walked so many times between Woolstaston and Ratlinghope is owned today by the National Trust. It remains common land over which the surrounding farmers have common rights to graze their sheep and ponies, though very few ponies are now put on the hill.

The National Trust ask that visitors adhere to the established public rights of way and the permissive paths that have been recently created when walking over the hill. The network is extensive and covers each of the main valleys. This will help to prevent erosion of the very shallow soil and reduce disturbance to the wildlife for which the Long Mynd is designated as a Site of Special Scientific Interest. The Trust has published an Access Map to the Long Mynd showing clearly all the designated routes.

Visitors to the area are advised to start their exploration from the Carding Mill Valley, where there is ample car parking as well as information, cafe and shop. Carr would still recognise parts of the scene though the cottages from which his rescuers came and the mill building itself have been demolished.

Obviously it would be foolhardy to try and retrace Carr's wanderings. The descents he described would be be even more dangerous in summer without a protective covering of snow. However there is a path up to the Light Spout waterfall from the Carding Mill Valley. The bridleway straight up the Carding Mill Valley is known as Dr Mott's Path after another professional who frequently had to cross the hill in the course of his duties, and was probably the surgeon summoned to treat Carr at the Crown Inn.

The way Carr followed before getting lost, between Ratlinghope and Robin Hood's Butts is accessible as a footpath. To complete a pleasant circular walk, turn off in the opposite direction to Carr's error, skirting the edge of Betchcott Hill and joining the Shropshire Way which goes via Lower Darnford to Ratlinghope as marked on the map on page 16.